# SUNSHINE AND SHADOW

poetry
by
Theresa E. Tilghman

**DORRANCE & COMPANY, INCORPORATED**
**828 LANCASTER AVENUE • BRYN MAWR, PENNSYLVANIA 19010**
*Publishers Since 1920*

Copyright © 1984 by Theresa E. Tilghman
*All Rights Reserved*
ISBN 0-8059-2932-0
Printed in the United States of America
*First Printing*

Dedicated to
All those who through the years have
touched my life and
enriched it,
and helped me to grow.

# Contents

| | |
|---|---|
| Foreword | vii |
| Passing of the Old Year | 1 |
| My Sister | 2 |
| The Parting | 3 |
| *En Passant* | 4 |
| Attainment | 5 |
| To My Wife | 6 |
| Transition | 7 |
| Contentment | 8 |
| Farewell, Little Sweetheart | 8 |
| The Kidnapped Babe | 9 |
| Thanksgiving | 10 |
| Dilemma | 10 |
| Finis | 11 |
| Thelma | 12 |
| My Haven | 14 |
| Rosie Anne | 15 |
| Shadows | 16 |
| My Sympathy | 17 |
| The Samaritans | 18 |
| Voice of His People | 19 |
| Three Sisters | 20 |
| Sunshine and Shadow | 21 |
| Her Day Was Done | 22 |
| Keeping Watch | 23 |
| Welcome, Old Age | 24 |
| He Giveth His Beloved Sleep | 25 |
| The Royal Wedding | 26 |
| The Victory Ride | 28 |
| What Can I Take? | 30 |
| Not Sunset, But Dawn | 31 |

| | |
|---|---:|
| Early Teachings | 32 |
| Little Log Cabin on the Hill | 33 |
| A Verse of Tribute | 34 |
| Two Uniforms | 35 |
| Two Mothers | 36 |
| The Friendship Circle | 37 |
| The Young Cowboy | 38 |
| The Preakness Ball | 39 |
| The Surgeon | 40 |
| Your Wedding Day | 41 |
| Ward Nurse | 42 |
| I Love the Severn | 43 |
| Homecoming | 44 |
| Gracious Lady of Weems Manor | 45 |
| Ode to Spring | 46 |
| On Your Wedding Day | 47 |
| Goodbye | 48 |
| Unexpressed | 49 |
| Faith | 49 |
| Then . . . And Now | 50 |
| Lauraville Church | 51 |
| Up Again! | 52 |
| The End of the Rainbow | 52 |
| Memorial Day, 1966 (A Parody) | 53 |
| On Retirement | 54 |
| Two Little Girls | 55 |
| Heart to Heart | 56 |
| What Shall We Plant? | 56 |

# Foreword

Many of these poems were written upon request, many from incidents, and others from imagination:

"Passing of The Old Year," "Thanksgiving," "Three Sisters," and "Ode to Spring"—written at various times while babysitting three little girls of the family with whom I boarded.

"The Parting"—for my mother-in-law on the death of her husband.

"The Kidnapped Babe"—on the kidnapping of the Lindbergh baby.

"Dilemma"—concerning two people I worked with.

"Finis"—on the death of President Coolidge, January, 1933.

"Thelma"—from the book by Marie Corelli.

"My Sympathy"—for my friend, Hilda Ray, on the death of her husband.

"The Samaritans"—in grateful remembrance of my friends, Miss Lizzie and Mr. George Bond.

"Voice of His People"—for King Albert of Belgium. Acknowledgement from the Lord Chancellor to the Queen, February, 1934.

"The Royal Wedding"—on the marriage of princess Marina of Greece to the Duke of Kent, 1934 (formal acknowledgement was received).

"A Verse of Tribute"—on the death of King George V of England, February, 1936. Acknowledged by private secretary to the King (King Edward VIII).

"Her Day Was Done"—for Mr. Ben Doggett of Weems, Virginia at the request of a friend on the death of his wife. I was told that he carried the poem in his wallet as long as he lived.

"He Giveth His Beloved Sleep"—in memory of a friend.

"The Victory Ride"—obviously no poem had as yet been written on that ride by Washington's Aide-de-Camp, Col. Tench Tilghman.

"Not Sunset, But Dawn"—the motto of the 1935 graduating class of Kilmarnock High School in Virginia. My niece, Jeanette Sickel, was one of the graduates and asked me to write the poem.

"The Little Log Cabin on the Hill"—pleasant memories of our visits to Aunt Lillie's log cabin on the Severn River, Maryland.

"The Friendship Class"—by request.

"The Surgeon"—for Dr. Reid Edwards, my surgeon in 1944.

"Ward Nurse"—for one of the nurses, 1944

"Homecoming"—at the request of Reverend Hudson to be read at a luncheon, Fruitland, Maryland.

"Gracious Lady of Weems Manor"—for Mrs. Olds, 1957, Weems, Virginia.

"Then ... And Now"—on the death of my husband in 1947.

"Lauraville Church"—by request for the fiftieth anniversary of the Church.

"Memorial Day, 1966"—I was the tenth girl.

"On Retirement"—by request and was read at Mr. Pease's retirement luncheon, Maryland Department of Motor Vehicles.

"Two Little Girls"—on my two granddaughters.

# PASSING OF THE OLD YEAR

The Old Year passes swiftly away,
    The New Year comes with the break of day;
E'en while I muse in the chimney nook,
    Time closes forever the Old Year book.

As I look back through the past I see
    Both sorrow and joys that have come to me;
I would not call thee back, oh no;
    Thou must be forgotten—'tis better so.

For who would recall the sorrow and pain?
    Treasure the sunshine, forget the rain.
We should be strengthened by our trials—
    Our lives are brightened by friendship's smiles.

We'll usher in the glad New Year
    But for the old one drop a tear;
For even as the year has flown,
    We, too, must pass to our eternal home.

# MY SISTER

Long ago I had a sister,
    My confidante and friend;
I thought nothing could part us
    Until the whole world's end.

My sister was much older,
    And I thought very wise;
My childish fears were vanquished
    By the love light in her eyes.

One night my sister left me
    On a journey dark and lone;
I could not bear her companie—
    She went to her Father's home.

My task I have not finished,
    My work on earth not done,
But when it is we'll meet again
    At the setting of the sun.

# THE PARTING

My husband you have gone from me—
    God called, you had to go;
His ways just now we cannot see
    But some day we shall know.

The years we've spent together
    Are a memory, I am alone;
But I know you are safe forever
    Within the Master's home.

We had no word of warning,
    You did not say farewell;
But the sorrow caused by your going
    No paltry words can tell.

No human voices now can reach
    The one we held most dear,
But the love of God can span the breach
    And keep us ever near.

# EN PASSANT

I loved you most sincerely,
    But you cast my love aside
And valued me most lightly
    Since I became your bride.

You have left me for another,
    The court has set you free;
And though you are her lover,
    Your vows were made to me.

But she who breaks the sacred ties
    Between a man and wife
And wins him with deceit and lies
    Will live no happy life.

She will not make you happy—
    You will realize too late
How true I was, how false she is,
    You'll rue your own mistake.

# ATTAINMENT

The girl could sing and she wished to sing
    For the music-loving masses.
She used to skip her daily school
    To go to vocal classes.

Her father gave her money,
    "Go purchase some new clothes."
But is that where the money went?
    Perhaps her teacher knows.

She sacrificed some pleasures
    (It was a worthy cause);
She had sung before the thousands
    And heard their great applause.

If we wish some bright vision,
    Some dear dream to come true,
We must sacrifice most nobly
    And labor for it, too.

# TO MY WIFE

We two were pals together
    In childhood long ago,
In time of sunny weather
    Or days of wintry snow.

When I had grown to manhood
    You, too, had not stood still;
And my kiss upon your forehead
    Brought an unaccustomed thrill.

We sat in the moonlit garden
    In apple blossom time;
I softly asked a question
    And you placed your hand in mine.

We are travelling down life's pathway,
    My hair is silvery white;
But to me you will always be as dear
    As you were our betrothal night.

# TRANSITION

I gaze in the sky at evening
    And I know the end is near,
But my trust alone is in Jesus—
    Of death I have no fear.

For He who loved the sinner
    Has washed me white as snow,
And if it's His voice calling,
    I'm satisfied to go.

I am loath to leave my loved ones,
    But I know it's not for long;
And at the resurrection
    We will join the ransomed throng.

Death has great compensation—
    In Heav'n there'll be no pain;
And after a short separation
    We shall meet our own again.

For He who loved the sinner
    Has washed me white as snow;
I know it's His voice calling,
    I'm satisfied to go.

# CONTENTMENT

I'd rather be poor and be happy
    Than have the wealth of the seas
With a burdened heart in my bosom
    Or a body that's wracked by disease.

For what is the wealth of the nation
    If health is not also thine own?
'Tis not to be had for the asking
    Nor bought by a king on his throne.

Let's not waste a moment repining,
    But always be pleasant and gay;
And as to success we are climbing—
    Do something for someone each day.

# FAREWELL, LITTLE SWEETHEART

Fare you well, my little darling,
    'Tis your wish I leave your side;
And you're planning in the future
    To become another's bride.

Au revoir, my brown-eyed sweetheart,
    Au revoir, but not goodbye.
Though the ocean rolls between us,
    I will love you till I die.

When in time you need a friend
    (For your lover is not true),
If to me a word you'll send,
    I will then return to you.

Then you'll realize my friendship
    And return my love sincere;
We'll be happy ever after
    In my cottage Windermere.

# THE KIDNAPPED BABE

O'er all the world has echoed
    The crime that has been done;
The parents searched for two long months
    To find their little son.

Their hearts were torn with anguish,
    Uncertain of his fate,
But when their only child was found,
    Alas, it was too late.

You heeded not the warning:
    "Harm not these little ones."
But to such fiends for crimes like this
    A time of reckoning comes.

# THANKSGIVING

Thanksgiving Day is drawing nigh
    With cranberry sauce and pumpkin pie;
The turkey's in the oven, brown,
    The children dancing all around.

Long years ago a Pilgrim band
    Braved dangers great to reach our land;
When anchored safe they knelt to pray—
    That was our first Thanksgiving Day.

For twelve months' hard and honest toil
    Rewards were great from the virgin soil.
Someone suggested, and they all said, "Aye,
    We'll name a special Thanksgiving Day."


# DILEMMA

She is just a little service clerk,
    Works at the W.U.,
Who twined herself around my heart
    And learned to love me, too.

Her mother says that Irish
    With Hebrew must not wed,
And that she cannot marry me,
    But this is what I said:

"Though different faiths keep us apart,
    Forever true I'll be;
Perhaps some day, who now can say?
    My love may come to me."

# FINIS

Our people pause to mourn today
    The passing of a life
Which held a firm and steady way
    'Midst all the toil and strife.

He ruled with wise and quiet hand
    The business of a nation;
He bowed not to a little band
    Nor courted great ovation.

He felt his task was finished,
    His earthly work was done,
His hold on life relinquished
    To meet his sainted son.

# THELMA

The country of ancient Norway
    Is a land of snow and ice;
Lord Errington thought a visit there,
    For a change, would be rather nice.

So with his crew and a couple of friends
    In his yacht he sailed away
And reached the land of the midnight sun
    Just at the close of day.

He anchored his craft and stepped ashore
    To inspect the rugged skoal.
But hark! What's that? That wondrous voice
    He will hear while the ages roll!

She placed her wreath on a granite grave
    Containing sacred dust;
Her dearest treasure was in Heaven
    Untouched by moth or rust.

Her melody was a sacred song
    To her mother's sainted spirit;
Her eyes were frightened like the fawn
    When it hears the hunter near it.

But Errington's reverent manner
    Soon put her fears at rest.
And she felt although an Englishman
    He must be one of the best.

The midnight sun shone down
    In all it's glory rare,
Enhancing the beauty of Thelma
    With her lovely golden hair.

She led him to her father's home
    And bade him step inside;
The two had lived there all alone
    Since Thelma's mother died.

Jarl Guldmar made him welcome
    As he rose from his big armchair—
A kindly man with clear blue eyes
    And snow-white beard and hair.

Lord Errington lingered many a day
    By the Altenfjord coast,
And when 'twas time to go away
    Fair Thelma's heart was lost.

But Errington loved her truly,
    To him she was a queen—
More full of grace and fair of face
    Than all he had ever seen.

And seeing their great happiness
    Old Guldmar hid his pain
And gave his treasure to the nobleman
    O'er his heart and home to reign.

# MY HAVEN

We strive to climb the enchanted stair
    Of glory, fame or wealth,
Yet who can be more rich than he
    Who has his work and health?

My castle is a six-room house
    With sunflowers 'round the door;
But Oh, what joy for me it holds
    When the busy day is o'er!

Two sprites meet me with laughing eyes
    And cheeks that are all aglow;
Then the queen of this small realm I spy,
    My friend through weal or woe.

I envy no man's riches,
    For I am richly blest
When I'm alone in my little home
    With those whom I love best.

# ROSIE ANNE

When the orange blossoms bloom in Maryland
    Down on the Eastern Shore,
I will leave it nevermore
    For I'm going back to marry Rosie Anne.

Guess they think that I'm a woman-hating man;
    But the girls of Baltimore
Can't compare with Easter Shore,
    So I'm going back to blue-eyed Rosie Anne.

When the robins start to sing in Maryland,
    And it's early in the spring,
Then the wedding bells will ring
    For I'm going back to marry Rosie Anne.

## SHADOWS

When the sun shone on the mountains
    And the clouds had passed from view,
I was walking in the Valley
    Of the Roses, dear, with you.

In my heart was naught of sorrow
    As you lingered by my side
For I thought upon the morrow
    To become your happy bride.

But the wedding bells were silent
    For they did not ring for me;
Now I wander sad and lonely,
    By the wild and restless sea.

Dearest schoolmate of my childhood
    Came and stole your love away;
From my life has gone the sunshine
    And I'm growing old and gray.

But I pray you both are happy,
    Journeying onward, side by side,
And think kindly of the maiden
    Who can never be your bride.

# MY SYMPATHY

On your father's arm eight years ago
    You walked up this same aisle;
On your golden hair was the bridal wreath,
    On your lips, a bride's shy smile.

He proudly gave you to his friend
    Who had won your girlish love;
You were made as one "till life shall end
    And God calls one above."

Again your father leads you,
    Today with measured tread,
To bid goodbye at the altar
    To one whom the world calls dead.

May the happy years together
    You spent as man and wife
Help make your tears less bitter
    As you face your future life.

The love and sympathy of friends
    Is sweet but can't allay
Our grief or loss when one so dear
    From us has passed away.

There's only One—the God of love—
    Can dry the widow's tears;
Through His grace we'll meet in the Home above
    To live through endless years.

# THE SAMARITANS

In a big brick house on Broadway
    They lived there all alone;
Brother and sister, comrades still,
    The others had passed on.

The rooms were still and silent,
    No childish laughter there;
No little feet heard pattering
    Upon the oaken stair.

Among the city's masses,
    The ceaseless din and roar,
Came a little country lassie
    Fresh from the Eastern Shore.

Her hair was not so curly,
    Her face was rather plain,
So no one bothered who she was
    Nor asked her whence she came.

But these two goodly people
    Saw the frankness of her eye,
Gave of their store of Christian love
    To the girl so strange and shy.

The years have flown, and the country maid,
    If asked, will tell you how
She made her way o'er a stony road
    (She is independent now).

Her dearest friends on earth today
    And those most tried and true
Are the two who first befriended her
    In her shabby coat of blue.

# VOICE OF HIS PEOPLE

Our King is dead. We will not hear
    His pleasant voice again.
The sport he loved has cost us dear—
    The people of his reign.

We gaze upon the beloved face
    As he lies in state awhile.
We will always carry in our hearts
    The memory of his smile.

We pledge allegiance to the one
    Who now ascends the throne
And his lovely wife, as fair a queen
    As e'er the sun shone on.

A noble son will take his place
    To reign in his father's stead;
May he guard the welfare of his race
    And by God's hand be led.

# THREE SISTERS

Three little sisters once there were
    In the town of Lauraville,
And I guess if they've not moved away
    They probably live there still.

The oldest one was Bernice;
    There was a Marjorie too;
The youngest one was Catherine
    With eyes of violet blue.

Bernice loved her kittens,
    She thought them simply grand,
And with all them and her radio
    She was the happiest girl in the land.

Marjorie was a lively one
    With pleasant voice and smile;
She spread good cheer where'er she went
    And made life seem worthwhile.

Now you, my little children,
    Can help spread sunshine too,
And the joy you give to others
    Will return threefold to you.

# SUNSHINE AND SHADOW

When the sun is low in the heavens
    We have to look up for the glow
That comes to those on the mountains
    But not in the vale below.

For earth is full of shadows,
    And oftentimes the sun
Seems not to find an object
    Till the day is almost done.

Behind the frown of the darkest cloud
    We often find God's smile,
And we shall enjoy the mountain more
    For being in the vale awhile.

Though our days may be filled with longing
    And our prayers unanswered still,
At the last comes a sweet contentment
    If we do our Master's will.

# HER DAY WAS DONE

Heart was weighted down with sorrow,
    Saw so many loved ones go,
And the sun of each tomorrow
    Brought no surcease of her woe.

Living on, but ever dreaming
    Of the son and daughter dear
That to her had been such blessings
    Filling home with love and cheer.

Dishes washed and rooms all dusted,
    Setting was the autumn sun;
Lay she down her earthly burdens
    When the quiet day was done.

# KEEPING WATCH

I lived in single blessedness
    For almost forty years;
Then we had one week of happiness
    'Ere my smiles were changed to tears.

There seemed no cloud of discontent
    In our matrimonial sky
For you, to all purposes and intent,
    Seemed quite as happy as I.

When you left home for work one day
    And kissed me a fond goodbye,
I never thought before your return
    Two long years would pass by.

For you my heart is yearning,
    You kiss me when I sleep;
So I'll keep the home fires burning,
    And my heart its faith will keep.

# WELCOME, OLD AGE

I early learned the social ropes
    And followed fashion's sway
With every moment occupied
    Throughout the livelong day.

The little things that in my youth
    Would vex my soul to tears
Now make me smile. There's much forsooth
    We learn with passing years.

For the world is just a great playhouse
    And "we the players all";
But I'm retiring from the stage
    'Ere the final curtain call.

I've played my part for sixty years,
    Well satisfied am I
To sit outside the footlights now
    And watch the show go by.

## HE GIVETH HIS BELOVED SLEEP

The dying rose upon her breast,
    The lamplight on her hair—
A beauteous form in shrouding dress,
    Sweet flowers perfume the air.

I enter in with silent tread
    The room made sacred now
By the presence of my beloved dead—
    I kiss the cold white brow.

She does not heed my tears and grief,
    Those eyes are closed for aye,
But a smile still lingers on the lips
    As loath to pass away.

She fell asleep. There is no death
    For those who serve our God;
And only a shell, not the lovely soul,
    Shall rest beneath the sod.

# THE ROYAL WEDDING

All England takes a holiday,
    The bells of London ring,
For this is the happy wedding day
    Of the son of England's King.
The lovely Princess Marina
    Has left her home and land
To wed the handsome nobleman
    Who has won her heart and hand.

From tens of thousands on the street
    Bursts forth a mighty cheer
When they see the glittering coaches
    Of the royal folk draw near.
I cannot see the bridal pair
    Nor yet the cheering throng,
But o'er the ocean, through the air,
    Comes the beautiful wedding song.

On the old Westminster organ
    Is played the wedding march,
And the Princess, on the arm of her father,
    Passes 'neath the flowery arch.
Westminster Abbey is crowded—
    They have come from far and wide
To witness the wedding of the two
    Who are Greece's and England's pride.

The organ now is silent,
    The marriage service is read;
He accepts her hand from her father
    And the minister bows his head.
He prays God's blessing upon them
    That are now made husband and wife,
And that He may always guide them
    Through the vicissitudes of life.

Their future looks ever so pleasant—
    They will live in a Prince's Hall;
But alike on peer and peasant
    The cloak of grief may fall.
So while the great of nations
    Are wishing them joy today,
We, too, pray God may keep them
    In peace and love alway.

# THE VICTORY RIDE

At the side of his commander
    As he was in every fray,
Was the faithful aide-de-camp
    On that great, immortal day.

When our troops marched into Yorktowne
    With the stars and stripes held high,
Cornwallis knew he must lower his flag
    Or see his soldiers die.

Down came the flag of England,
    Up went the flag of white:
The Colonies had conquered—
    Their cause was just and right.

To the Continental Congress
    The word of peace must go;
When Tilghman crossed the river
    The sun was sinking low.

From the Eastern Shore on horseback
    The ride was lone and long,
But his brave heart never faltered
    And he sang a cheering song.

"The British have surrendered,
    The bloody war is o'er;
No more will we from slumber
    Awake to the cannons' roar."

Thus he called out to the people,
    Speeding onward through the night,
And at two o'clock one morning
    Philadelphia was in sight.

People wakened from their slumber,
    Thought he surely was insane,
But their anger changed to gladness
    When they knew why Tilghman came.

Famous ride of Paul Revere
    Fills the schoolboy's heart with pride,
But 'twas left to an unknown poet
    To portray Tench Tilghman's ride!

# WHAT CAN I TAKE?

What can I take along with me
    When I start the downward trail?
When I've passed the crest and paused to rest,
    And the noonday sun grows pale?
We can only take the things we have prized
    Throughout life's changing day;
We cannot clasp with one quick grasp
    The things we have cast away.

But these things I can take with me
    When I've crossed the mountain's height—
Though the way be drear while I tarry here
    They illumine my soul with light:
My faith in Christ who died for me
    Because of his wondrous love,
That a child of sin might enter in
    The realms of joy above.

I shall take the first sweet baby smile
    Of my one and only son;
My soul it will cheer when I shrink with fear
    And the shades of night come on.
I shall take the sound of a silvery laugh
    And a picture of twinkling eyes,
When my work was done, and I came home
    To my son, and paradise.

I shall take the clasp of two little arms—
    My darling's goodnight kiss;
I still can hear, "Goodnight, Mother dear,"
    What sweeter memory than this?
I shall take the love and friendships true
    That have lightened life's heavy load;
These things I shall keep 'til I fall asleep
    When I've come to the end of the road.

# NOT SUNSET, BUT DAWN

Not sunset, but dawn
    Our schooldays are past;
The friendships of years—
    How long will they last?
Not sunset, but dawn
    Graduation has come,
Out into the world
    We each go alone.

Not sunset, but dawn
    Wherever we go
We will look back with joy
    On our schooldays I know.
Not sunset, but dawn
    We now bid adieu
To teachers and schoolmates
    Both loyal and true.

Not sunset, but dawn
    May the future be bright;
May we ever be guided
    By the only true Light.
And when the full length
    Of life's journey we've gone,
Remember it's still
    Not sunset, but dawn.

# EARLY TEACHINGS

What! Not look on death
    That is so intertwined with life?
Dost thou not know the last faint breath
    Oft ends a toilsome strife?

He is too young to look on death?
    Oh no, it cannot be,
For oftentimes God calls one home
    That is younger yet than he.

He will not be afraid of one
    Who thought so much of him;
She even spoke of my little son
    When the light was growing dim.

I tell him God was sorry
    Her sufferings were so great,
And now her husband welcomes her
    Inside the golden gate.

I would early teach this child of mirth
    That everyone must die,
And death is only a natural birth
    To a life beyond the sky.

# THE LITTLE LOG CABIN ON THE HILL

We took a ride on Sunday
    Away from the city's roar,
And rode along for an hour or so
    'Til we glimpsed the Severn's shore.
We knelt down by a huckleberry bush
    To drink from a sparkling rill,
But the sight which charmed my tired eyes most
    Was the little log cabin on the hill.

I found some green arbutus
    That was trailing on the ground,
Although it was almost covered
    By leaves that feel around.
I took some roots of it home with me—
    It seems to be living still—
And when I look at it I see
    The little log cabin on the hill.

I want a cabin like this—
    When my day's work is done
I'll sit outside the doorway
    And watch the setting sun.
In the heavenly peace and beauty
    I'll obey my Master still,
And when he calls I'll answer
    From the little log cabin on the hill.

## A VERSE OF TRIBUTE

Walk softly, all ye people,
    Highborn and lowly too,
For here was a mighty monarch
    That to his trust was true.

His death is mourned from coast to coast
    Of the English-speaking world;
Beloved was he where'er you see
    The British flag unfurled.

He lived an active, useful life
    And was only seventy-one,
But the Master of the vineyard
    Proclaimed, "Thy work is done."

In the solemn hush of midnight
    With loved ones gathered near,
His soul took flight to the land of light
    And left them mourning here.

How dolefully the churchbell rings,
    The lights are all made dim;
He has gone to meet the King of Kings,
    And his works live after him.

# TWO UNIFORMS

Always on Memorial Day
    She opens a little chest,
Takes out a coat of faded gray,
    The trousers and a vest.

She lays aside with reverent hands
    The symbol of defeat;
Then looks upon another suit
    Of khaki, pressed and neat.

The last is only a cowboy suit,
    Her son's pride as a child;
She has no uniform he wore
    In that conflict, fierce and wild.

Years after the Civil War was o'er
    Her father died at home;
But her firstborn fell on a foreign shore
    In the battle of Argonne.

She visits every loved one's "bed,"
    Putting flowers on each one,
And lays two wreaths on her father's grave,
    But one is for her son.

# TWO MOTHERS

Johnny's mother primps her hair,
    An' fixes up her face;
It looks like she's acopyin'
    The 'Merican Indian race.
His mother's always busy
    Goin' to clubs and things,
An' boys don't she look ritzy
    With all 'em diamon' rings!

The maid puts him to bed at night
    An' tends to him all day;
His mother don't have any time
    To talk to him or play!
My mother don't need any paint
    'Cause she plays ball with me,
An' her cheeks are jes' as rosy
    As ever they can be!

Her dresses might not cost so much
    'Cause we're not rich, you see,
But when she an' Dad get all dressed up
    They look okay to me.
'Spec' Johnny's folks are very nice,
    But I guess I wouldn't trade—
My mom and dad are real pals,
    The best 'at was ever made!

# THE FRIENDSHIP CIRCLE

Standing outside the church one day
    I heard a young lady to another one say,
"One class is young, one is too old,
    Girls my age are left out in the cold."

So we started to arrange with right good will
    A brand new class at Lauraville;
Some brought two, some brought one,
    And the Friendship Circle was begun.

The Friendship Circle should thrive forsooth
    With secretary Dorothy and President Ruth.
Mildred and Pearle—what would we do
    without this helpful, inseparable two?

Helen and Leila, Antoinette and Em,
    Edna and Lola, don't forget them.
Also the teacher with her pleasant smile—
    The example she sets is quite worthwhile.

'Tis a splendid class and we hope to hear
    Of them bringing new members from far and near.
May each light shine brightly, be it great or small,
    And God's rich blessing shall be over all.

# THE YOUNG COWBOY

I'm all dressed up from hat to boot
    When I put on my cowboy suit;
I see nothing close at hand
    I'm down in Texas by the Rio Grande.

'Round my neck a kerchief, on my hip a gun,
    Living in the saddle from sun to sun.
My heart is light and free from care
    As I go riding through the keen fresh air.

Down by the river 'neath a shady tree
    Is the best lunch table there is for me;
And when I've finished I'm up and away
    In my saddle again 'til the end of the day.

# THE PREAKNESS BALL

Gone now is winter's bleakness,
    There's spring in the hearts of all,
For tomorrow is the day of the Preakness,
    And tonight is the Preakness Ball.

Maryland races twice a year—
    In the springtime and the fall;
And the great event in the month of May
    Is the Preakness and the Ball.

Line up the Maryland beauties
    As fair as ever seen;
Now comes the pleasant duty
    Of choosing the Preakness Queen.

For grace and beauty of renown
    Beloved by one and all,
Fair Mrs. Lanahan is crowned
    The Queen of the Preakness Ball.

# THE SURGEON

Deep the furrows of his forehead
    And the lines of mouth are grim;
But you wonder why unpleasant
    Things of life have bothered him.

Lovely home and happy family—
    It would seem that such as he
Would be Fortune's favored children,
    Preconceived by destiny.

But the clear eyes of the surgeon
    Seem to glow with inner light
As he deftly wields the scalpel
    To correct disease's blight.

God has given him the skill—
    Far beyond our common ken;
Of his gift he freely gives
    To his suffering fellowmen.

## YOUR WEDDING DAY

The parties now are over
    The happy day has come;
Two single lives shall be no more,
    They're united into one.

The future lies before you
    And today you cannot know
The sunshine or the shadows
    On the path that you will go.

But faith has a way of opening
    Many a tight-closed door;
And love can lighten the burden
    That seemed so heavy before.

So here's a toast to the bride and groom,
    And a wish worth more than gold—
'Tis only this: May your love increase
    As the future years unfold.

# WARD NURSE

She comes tripping down the hall,
    And her pleasant southern drawl
Chases shadows from their place of deepest
    gloom;
    And her merry, cheery smile,
As she's working all the while,
    Seems to brighten every corner of the room.

She comes in and makes your bed,
    Rubs your back and bathes your head—
She'll do anything she can to humor you;
    She's the girl from Carolina,
And you'll never find a finer
    Or a better little nurse than Fanny Lou!

# I LOVE THE SEVERN

I love the Severn in the twilight
    When the sun is sinking to rest
And, painting the sky with color,
    Makes a rainbow of the west.

I love the Severn in the evening
    When, save for the whippoorwills' call
And the ripple of the wavelets,
    Sweet silence broods over all.

I love the Severn by moonlight
    With the pinetrees 'gainst the sky,
Like the spirits of the dear departed
    Keeping watch o'er you and I.

I love the Severn when the moonlight
    Pours down in a golden stream,
Changing the water to silver
    And life into a dream.

## "HOMECOMING"

I am going back today
    To that church so far away
Where we gathered Sunday mornings, years ago;
    Folks will come from far and near,
And my heart is filled with cheer
    As I think of seeing those I used to know.

Culver, Toadvine, Pryor, and Brown—
    Each a family of renown
Who've been faithful to the church for many years;
    Older ones have passed away,
But the members of today
    Still come here and share their mutual smiles and tears.

Layfield, Hobbs, and Livingston
    Are some families who will come;
Farlows, Dykes, and Tilghmans will be present too;
    What a grand "homecoming" this—
Foretaste of a greater bliss
    When we gather 'round the throne beyond the blue.

Gentle Shepherd of us all
    Is the one who heard the call,
Living as a youth upon his father's farm;
    In the twilight years ahead
May he by God's hand be led,
    Safely kept by Him from every harm.

# GRACIOUS LADY OF WEEMS MANOR

A stately lady of eighty-eight—
    Enriched are all who enter her gate.
I came to her house at another's request;
    She opened to us her treasure chest
Of memories rich in historic lore,
    And romance, too, a goodly store.
She dreams of the past, but lives today,
    And captures the beauty that comes her way.

The beauty of sky and sea and land
    Appears on canvas 'neath her gifted hand.
She thanks her Lord for food and health,
    Family and friends—intrinsic wealth.

In an era of turmoil and discontent
    Such a happy soul seems heaven sent.
To us of younger, unfinished mold
    She teaches the art of growing old.

# ODE TO SPRING

No more skating on the river,
    No more sledding down the hill,
And the wild geese have gone northward
    From the pond at Parker's mill.
Now the sun shines somewhat brighter,
    And the days are getting long,
And the trees shoot forth their leaflets,
    And the world bursts into song.

When the crocus starts to peeping
    Through the grass upon the hill,
And "Virginia" starts to creeping
    Beside the rocky rill;
Then the robin starts to chirping
    And the mockingbird to sing—
Everywhere there's joy and gladness,
    And we know that it is Spring!

## ON YOUR WEDDING DAY

On this lovely day in April
    Friends have come from far and near
To be witness to the union
    Of the two they hold so dear.

Overhead the birds are singing,
    Under foot the flowers gay
Nod their heads as if they're saying,
    "Happy, happy Wedding Day."

Now your love, each for the other,
    Like your rings is very new;
And the pathways of the future
    Will be testing grounds for you.

But with faith and hope to strengthen,
    Patience, too, for every need,
Love will find a way to conquer
    All the things that growth impede.

Midst the joyous talk and laughter,
    Cheery wishes, ringing true
Is the prayer that God may guide you
    All the wondrous journey through.

# GOODBYE

There's an aching void in my heart for you
    And yet I cannot cry;
I never knew when we said goodnight
    That it would be goodbye.

"Au revoir, Adios, I'll see you, So long,"
    And a tear may bedim the eye;
But the saddest word in any tongue
    Is the single word Goodbye.

Oh, why must I always say farewell
    To the ones I hold most dear—
They move away, or there comes a day
    When I stand beside their bier.

But the time will come when we all reach Home
    In that land beyond the sky;
All partings are o'er on that other shore
    And we'll nevermore say goodbye.

## UNEXPRESSED

If I could write a beautiful song
    To live long after I am gone,
'Twould make me happy along the way
    And bring me joy at the close of life's day.

My fingers never could touch the keys
    To bring forth beautiful melodies;
My lips could never speak the thought
    That the simple joy of living brought.

For life is a gift from God above—
    Earthly flower of Heavenly love;
And though the flower will fade away
    'Twill bloom again to live alway.

## FAITH

Let not the shade of rampant doubts
    Bedim my tranquil sky,
For only those do truly live
    Who aren't afraid to die!

# THEN ... AND NOW

I wrote a song when a stranger died—
    The mourners I never knew;
But it touched an answering chord in my heart,
    As these things sometimes do.

I wrote a song when my teacher died,
    A woman whom all did love;
It turned our thoughts from her sad home here
    To the Heavenly one above.

I wrote a song when a friend passed on,
    A friend we held most dear;
It helped to cheer the saddened heart
    And check the falling tear.

But I could not write a song for you—
    My brain and pen are still;
You answered to the call of God—
    I yield me to His will.

# LAURAVILLE CHURCH

Midst a scene of verdant beauty
    Stood the Little Eutaw church;
Songs of service, faith, and duty
    Echoed through the groves of birch.

Families came to church together,
    Casting off their fret and care;
Be it fair or stormy weather,
    Every Sunday found them there.

Messrs. Burton, Knox and Bing
    Living so far out the way
Thought 'twould be a spendid thing
    To build another church some day.

In the summer of nineteen four
    The "Tabernacle" was begun,
And in March of nineteen seven
    The new stone church was done.

But the congregation grew,
    People worked hard, one and all,
And in a few short years we knew
    The little stone church was far too small.

So the members looked around,
    Signs of future growth did heed,
And at length a site was found
    Large enough to fit the need.

From the chapel on the hill
    (Long since fallen to decay)
Came our church of Lauraville—
    "My word shall not pass away."

# UP AGAIN!

We will work a little faster,
    Raise our song up to the skies,
And we'll find that we can master
    Situations as they rise.

Life's not always easy sailing,
    There is poverty and pain,
Still, from every fall and failing
    We will rise and strive again.

In the field of sweetest clover
    There are always weeds and tares;
So in life the whole world over
    Joys are mingled with the cares.


# THE END OF THE RAINBOW

Let's take a trip together
    To the Land of Dreams Come True;
We'll brave the stormy weather
    And skies of darkest hue.

We'll pass by the way of yesterday
    And the mountain of broken dreams;
We'll find the dell where fairies dwell
    And the golden moonlight gleams.

We'll find the end of the rainbow
    Away from storm and stress,
Because at the end of the rainbow
    We'll find our happiness.

# MEMORIAL DAY, 1966

## (A Parody)

Listen, my children, and you shall hear
    The strangest story of the current year.

For twenty years, a little less,
    I'd been quite lonely, I will confess.
But I never thought of such a thing
    As having another romantic fling.

'Til one fine day, right out of the blue
    (Mildred can tell you my story is true),
By all nine women a man is seen
    Slowly crossing the lawn so green.

From eighteen years to sixty-six,
    Now which of them knew the latest tricks
To lure him from his lonely state
    And perhaps arrange a future date?

He was introduced, he looked around
    And pretty soon he sat him down.
He talked at length of this and that
    To the lady who nearest to him sat.

A week passed by and none of the ten
    Had seen or heard of the man again.
(There was one, by now you may have deduced,
    Wasn't there when the others were introduced.)

Then a few days later, one evening at home,
    The tenth girl answered the telephone.
The dates continue from then 'til now;
    They will end sometime, but who knows how?

Epiloque: May, 1967.

My poem now is finished, the story is done.
Was it fate from beginning? The gentleman has won.

## ON RETIREMENT

No more Friday bundles
    To go to Lutherville;
No more Monday morning blues,
    You sleep (or rise) at will.

No more smoky sessions
    And mumbling down the "board,"
Wondering which is nonsense
    And which you should record.

You'll miss Herr Bailey's doodles,
    Mcmullen's funny jokes,
And Claggett's sudden "Hold it!
    I'll go and see the folks!"

So here's to your retirement—
    Enjoy your well-earned ease;
But where will we find a man to fill
    The place of Mr. Pease?

# TWO LITTLE GIRLS

Two little girls we often see
    And love to "beat the band"—
One girl's name is Linda Marie,
    The other is Kimberly Anne.

Linda is only three-and-a-half,
    Kimberly a "little past two";
There's music in their silvery laugh
    Because it rings so true.

"Grandaddy, come and 'pank me!"
    Kimberly often calls;
She likes for him to tease her,
    Then she runs and almost falls.

They gambol with their Schottsie,
    He runs and turns and twirls;
Like us, he'd be a lonely one
    Without these two little girls.

# HEART TO HEART

In the springtime of our living
    We don't vision winter's cold;
And we seldom think of giving
    Part of Self to those grown old.

If, when I have grown much older,
    I can't see you standing there,
Come and touch me on the shoulder
    Just to let me know you care.

If my mind is blank to others
    And your words I cannot hear,
Press your lips upon my forehead
    And I'll know it's you, my dear.

Soon my journey will be ended,
    Though I don't know how or when,
But some day you'll come and join me,
    And we'll be together then.


# WHAT SHALL WE PLANT?

What shall we plant in the Garden of Life
    As we labor from day to day?
Shall we plant the seeds of envy and strife
    And thorns along the way?

No, I would plant the seeds of love
    And courage in the hearts of men;
Though the going be tough and you're down in the rough,
    You'll arise and try again.

Faith in God, transcending all,
    And faith in my fellowman;
The world is big, my part is small,
    But I'll do it the best I can.